SEVEN STORIES OF CHRISTMAS LOVE

SEVEN STORIES OF CHRISTMAS LOVE

LEO BUSCAGLIA

ILLUSTRATED BY TOM NEWSOM

The following stories have been previously published in *Woman's Day:*
"A Christmas Morning Memory"
"Two Festivals of Light"
"The Christmas Story According to Big Matthew"
"Christmas in Bali"
"The Christmas That Almost Wasn't"

Library of Congress catalog number: 87-042748
Slack, Incorporated ISBN: 1-55642-019-6
Henry Holt and Company, Inc. ISBN 0-8050-2434-4
Published in the United States of America by:
SLACK, Incorporated
6900 Grove Road
Thorofare, New Jersey 08086
In the United States, distributed to the trade by:
Henry Holt and Company, Inc.
115 West 18th Street
New York, New York 10011

In Canada, distributed to the trade by:
Fitzhenry & Whiteside Ltd.,
195 Allstate Parkway
Markham, Ontario L3R 4T8.

Printed in the United States of America
All first editions are printed on acid-free paper.∞

11   13   15   17   19   20   18   16   14   12   10

For my publisher and dear friend,
Charles Slack,
for all the Christmas
he has brought into my life

CONTENTS

INTRODUCTION

Christmas is the Christian celebration of the birth of Jesus, the Holy Child of Bethlehem, nearly two thousand years ago. But whatever your religious belief, the spirit of Christmas is love, and love is universal.

This book is a Christmas sharing. There are no villains mentioned here, no hard hearts, no skeptics. I have left this for others to write. This short work is for those who have no trouble accepting miracles, who don't require explanations, who still believe in love, generosity, devotion, goodness, and the wonder of life.

In an age dominated by science, with emphasis upon the actual and literal, we tend to scoff at dreams and miracles. Christmas encourages and reinforces these parts of our nature. It brings out the spirituality we sense within, conjures up images we know from memories too deeply a part of our universal consciousness to ever fade.

I have shared on these pages some personal memories of Christmases past. These memories are still so alive for me that they required little more than a moment's pause to recall them vividly, even though some of them happened many, many years ago.

It is my hope that those who will take the time to read these stories will themselves recollect their own Christmases past. Perhaps in this way, through the power of memory, they will recapture the feelings of joy, peace, love, and hope that the season is all about.

May your Christmas be full of love and bring you ever new and wondrous memories to use as sustenance for the years to come.

Life is so full of meaning and purpose
So full of beauty—beneath its covering
That you will find earth but cloaks your heaven.
Courage then to claim it; that is all!

—Fra Giovanni

A CHRISTMAS MORNING MEMORY

*Every choice we make
has its consequences.
No one fools the
Christmas Angel.*

I didn't believe her. Angels had better things to do with their time than watch to see if I was a good or bad boy. Even with my limited seven-year-old wisdom I had figured out that, at best, the Angel could only watch over two or three kids at a time . . . and why should I be one of them? The odds were certainly in my favor. Yet Mama, who knew all things, had told me, time and time again, that the Christmas Angel knew, saw, and evaluated all things and could not be compared with anything we ignorant human beings understood. Anyway, I wasn't at all sure that I believed in the Christmas Angel. All my friends in the neighborhood told me that it was Santa Claus who came on Christmas Eve and that they'd never heard of an angel who brought presents. Mama had lived in America for years and blessed her new land as her permanent home, but she was forever as Italian as polenta; and, for her, it would always be an angel. "Who's this Santa Claus?" she'd say. "And what has he to do with Christmas?"

In addition, I must admit that I wasn't too impressed with our Italian Angel. Santa Claus was always more generous and imaginative. He brought my friends bicy-

18

cles, Tinkertoys,® puzzles, candy canes, and baseball mitts. Italian Angels always brought apples, oranges, assorted nuts, raisins, a small panettone (cake), and some little round licorice candies we called *bottone di prete* (priest's buttons) because they looked like the buttons you'd find on a priest's cassock. Also, the Angel always included in our stockings some imported chestnuts, hard as rocks. I must admit I never understood what to do with the chestnuts. We finally gave them to Mama to be boiled into submission, then peeled and ate them for dessert after Christmas dinner. It hardly seemed a very appropriate gift for a child of six or seven. The Christmas Angel couldn't be too bright, I often thought.

When I questioned Mama about this, she would only say that it was not for me, "still wet behind the ears," to question an angel, especially the Christmas Angel.

During this particular Christmastime my seven-year-old behavior could hardly have been said to be exemplary. My brother and sisters, all older than I, never seemed to cause any problems. I, on the other hand, always seemed to be the center of them all. At mealtime I hated everything. I was required to take *un poco di tutto*, a bite of everything, and each meal became a challenge . . . Felice, as I was called by the family, against the world of adults. It was I who never remembered to close the

chicken coop, who would rather read than take out the garbage, and who, most of all, challenged everything that Mama and Papa did, felt, or commanded. In short, I was a brat.

For at least a month prior to Christmas, Mama warned me, "You're being a very bad boy, Felice. Christmas Angels don't bring presents to brats. They bring them a stick from a peach tree suitable for hitting on the legs. So," she alerted me, "you'd better change your ways. I can't be good for you. Only you can choose to be good."

"Who cares?" was my response. "The Angel never brings me anything I want anyway." I did very little over the next weeks toward "mending my ways."

As it is in most homes, Christmas Eve was a magical time. Even though we were very poor, we always had special foods to eat. After dinner we sat around the wood stove that served as the center of our lives during the winter months and talked and laughed and listened to stories. We would spend much time planning for the next day's feast, for which we had been preparing all week. Being a Catholic family, we would all go to confession, after which we'd decorate the tree. The evening would end with a small cup of Mama's wondrous zabaglione.

Never mind that it had some wine in it, Christmas came only once a year!

I'm sure that it is true of all children, but I found it almost impossible to get to sleep on Christmas Eve. My mind danced. Not with thoughts of sugarplums, but with serious concerns like the possibility that the Christmas Angel would miss my house or run out of gifts. I would become very excited over the possibility that Santa Claus would forget we were Italian and stop in anyway, not realizing that I had already been visited by the Angel. Then I'd get a double dose of everything!

How is it that Christmas morning, no matter how little sleep was had the night before, never presents a wake-up problem? So it was on this particular morning. It was just a matter of moments after hearing the first movement before we were all up and charging for the kitchen and the clothesline, on which were hanging our stockings and under which were our bright, newly polished shoes.

It was all as we had left it the night before except that the shoes and stockings were stuffed to capacity with the Christmas Angel's bounty—that is, all except mine. My shoes, shining brightly, were empty. My stockings, hanging loosely over the line, were equally empty except for one, from which emerged a long dry peach limb.

I saw the looks of horror on the faces of my brother and sisters. We all stopped in our tracks. All eyes went to Mama and Papa, then back again to me.

Mama said, "Ah, I knew it. The Christmas Angel never misses a thing. The Christmas Angel only leaves what we deserve."

My eyes welled up with tears. My sisters reached out to comfort me, but I fought them off savagely.

"I didn't want those dumb presents," I cried. "I hate the dumb old Angel. There's no Christmas Angel anyway."

I fell into Mama's arms. She was a large woman, and her lap had saved me from despair and loneliness so many times before. I saw that she was crying as she comforted me. So was Papa. My sisters' loud sobbing and my brother's sniffling filled the early-morning silence.

After a while my mother spoke, as if talking to herself. "Felice isn't a bad boy. He just acts bad from time to time. The Christmas Angel knows that. He could have been good if he wanted to, but this year he chose to be bad. There was nothing else the Angel could do. Maybe next year he'll decide to be better. But for now, we can all be happy again."

Everyone immediately emptied the gifts in their shoes and stockings onto my lap. "Here," they said, "take

this." Within a short while the house was again full of chatter, smiles, and laughter. I had received more than my shoes and stockings could ever carry.

Mama and Papa had gone to mass early, as usual. They had collected the chestnuts and set them on their way to hours of boiling in a wonderful spiced water—another pot among sauces simmering. Delicate odors emerged like magic potions from the oven, all on the way to becoming our miraculous Christmas dinner.

We all got ready for church. As was her usual practice, Mama checked each of us in turn: a collar adjusted here, hair pulled back there, a soft caress for each.

It was my turn last. She set her very large brown eyes on mine. "Felice," she said, "do you understand why the Christmas Angel couldn't leave you gifts?"

"Uh-huh," I answered.

"The Angel reminds us that we will always get what we deserve. We can't escape it. Sometimes it's hard to understand and it hurts and makes us cry. But it teaches us what's right and wrong, and we get better every year."

I'm not certain that at the time I really understood what she meant. I knew only that I was sure I was loved, that whatever I had done, I had been forgiven, and that there would always be another chance for me.

I have never forgotten that Christmas so many years ago. Since then life has not always been fair or offered me what I thought I'd deserved or rewarded my being good. Over the years I know that I have been selfish, bratty, thoughtless, and perhaps, at times, even cruel . . . but I have never forgotten that where there is forgiveness, sharing, another chance given, and unwavering love, the Christmas Angel is always present and it's always Christmas.

TWO FESTIVALS OF LIGHT

Love never dies
as long as there is someone
who remembers.

*C*hristmas never fails to evoke memories. Most of us can recall Christmases of great joy and of disappointment, of warm camaraderie and of frightening loneliness, of exciting hellos and of painful good-byes.

It's strange how memory works—why we remember what we remember and forget what we forget. How is it that I can remember so vividly the details of a special Christmas more than fifty years ago, and forget important events of just a few days past?

I could not have been more than eight or nine years old on the Christmas when our new neighbors moved in. It was an exceptionally cold and rainy Los Angeles December. I remember it well because of the embarrassment I felt over having to wear my sister's winter coat, which she had outgrown. In our home, clothes were not thrown out, they were handed down, and it was my turn—no matter the girlish fur piping on the collar and sleeves and buttons on the wrong side.

We lived in a small house heated by a single woodburning stove that served to separate the kitchen and the dining room. I remember how we huddled that December to dress by its heat. The house was frame, similar

to many others that are still to be found in the Boyle Heights area of Los Angeles. They were proudly referred to at the time as craftsman houses.

The families who lived on our street were mostly first-generation immigrants: Jews from Eastern Europe, Italians from southern Italy, Germans, and Mexicans. Few of them spoke much English, most had large families, all of them were poor.

Our new neighbors moved in early in December—a rabbi and his family: a boy, Elijah, who was my age, and a girl, Sarah, a few years older. When I saw them for the first time I pretended to be playing, but watched as their large old pieces of furniture were unloaded from the moving van and disappeared into the darkness behind their front door. I wondered what they'd be like, if they'd speak English, if they'd be friendly. As is usually the case under such circumstances, it was Elijah and I who were the first to talk. It always seems easier for children, for some reason. We were soon walking to school each day, fast becoming close friends. He was one of the few children who didn't laugh at my coat.

We were standing in the school yard waiting for the bell to ring one morning when the subject of the approaching holiday came up.

"What are you going to get for Christmas?" I asked Elijah.

"I don't believe in Christmas," he said simply.

I was stunned.

"Everybody believes in Christmas," I insisted.

"I'm Jewish. We don't," he answered matter-of-factly.

"Well, what do you believe in if you don't believe in Christmas?" I persisted.

"Lots of things. But not Christmas," he responded.

When something of any importance happened during the day in our lives, it was always shared with the family at our dinner table that evening. It was here that anxieties were lessened, mysteries solved, solutions arrived at. I couldn't wait to tell the startling news. Our new neighbors didn't believe in Christmas!

Mama and Papa were as mystified as I was at the news. They were not moved by my elder brother's explanation that Christmas is a religious holiday, that there are all kinds of beliefs in the world, that the Cohens had as much right not to believe in Christmas as we did to believe in it. After all, he reasoned further, wasn't that part of why so many people left their homelands to emigrate to the United States?

Mama in her innocent wisdom rationalized, "Maybe

they don't know about it. They come from far away, like we do, and maybe no one told them yet."

"Well, they don't come from the moon," my brother laughed.

"Don't be so smart," my mother said, "or I'll send *you* to the moon!" Mama had a way of making a point. She turned to Papa across the table. "They should be invited to share Christmas with us," she said.

That was Mama's way of handling any problem—feed it! And there was always a place at the table for anyone at any time. Perhaps that's why so many of my fondest memories are associated with eating.

Within a week of their moving in I was hired by Rabbi Cohen as their *Shabbes goy:* the Gentile who serves the family on their Sabbath. I was paid generously—a nickel a week for the job, a fortune for a poor kid at the time. It was very easy. I just had to turn on the lights when the family returned from the synagogue, move a few pots of food to the stove, and turn on the gas.

This, of course, became another mysterious subject for our table talk. "How come you have to do that? That's really strange."

A few weeks prior to Christmas I was serving the Cohens' Sabbath table. When I finished my ritual, I did as

I had been instructed by Papa and invited Rabbi Cohen and his family to Christmas dinner at our home. Elijah had warned me that they wouldn't come.

Rabbi Cohen was a man not easily forgotten. He was of medium stature but appeared much larger than life, with his bespectacled alert dark eyes, his shocking mass of black hair, his dark beard, and his black clothing—all serving to accentuate the whiteness of his delicate face and hands. We all thought that he was the very image of the man on the Smith Brothers cough drop box.

In his deep, melodious voice he answered my invitation. "Ah," he said. "Ve vould like to come to your house and meet your mama and papa, but better I talk first to your papa."

"They don't talk English too good," I warned him. "That's why they asked me to invite you. They talk Italian."

"Vell," the rabbi said with a smile, "I don't talk too good, either. But ve'll understand each other. Vy not? Ve're neighbors."

When he was at home Papa could always be found in his garden. Behind the house grew endless vegetables: onions, peppers, garlic, zucchini, carrots, lettuce, and whatever the seasonal vegetables or fruits were. The front of the house was always a profusion of flowers. It

was especially lovely this Christmas season, with large bushes of poinsettias—double red, in full bloom.

Rabbi Cohen stopped Papa at his weeding a few days later. Elijah and I, now good friends, stood close by to watch the historic encounter.

"I'm Rabbi Cohen, your new neighbor."

"I know you jus-a move in," Papa said. "Is-a good you jus-a move in."

"It's time ve should meet," Rabbi Cohen said, with his unique inflection. He shook Papa's hand warmly. "I vant to thank you for the invitation to be vis you and your family for Christmas dinner."

"It's-a all right," Papa said. "You and your family come. We gotta plenty to eat."

"That's a problem," the rabbi smiled. "You see, ve can only eat certain style foods. Ve run a kosher household."

"Well," said Papa, in the usual way he had of refusing to allow anything to present a problem. "We'll cook what-a you eat—kosher." Of course, Papa had no idea what kosher was. He was counting on Mama's usual creativity in the kitchen.

"Vell," replied Rabbi Cohen, "it's a little bit more complicated dan dat."

He proceeded to explain what a kosher household en-

tails. Papa nodded understanding, but it became plain that evening at the dinner table that he had understood very little of what the rabbi told him. What he concluded was that Jews ate differently from other people, that they did know what Christmas was all about, and that they too had a very special holiday in December called Hanukkah. But in spite of communication problems, Papa was delighted to tell us that the Cohens would be our guests for Christmas dinner and, in turn, we were invited to share their Hanukkah ceremony several nights later.

My elder sister was sent out to the nearby kosher market on Wabash and Evergreen with instructions to buy enough kosher food to satisfy at least ten people. Papa wanted to be sure there would be enough. Though we had very little money to spare, feeding our new neighbors was a very high priority.

My mother was delighted and intrigued when my sister returned with large bags of assorted foods in tightly sealed jars and containers marked "kosher." The grocer had helped her select a very special feast, indeed.

Both holiday visits were great successes. After surmounting various problems and supplying appropriate utensils of their own, the Cohens were very touched by the special dinner set before them. The Buscaglias de-

voured their Christmas feast with their accustomed gusto. There were gifts for the Cohens under the Christmas tree, and in the soft glow of Christmas lights we serenaded them with carols, in both English and Italian.

Each year Mama proudly displayed a traditional manger scene which was made up of several small hand-carved figures: Mary, Joseph, the infant Jesus, and a few shepherds, angels, and animals which she had managed to carry with her among the few possessions she brought from Italy. Over the manger was a tiny banner on which were printed the words *"Pace sulla terra agli uomini di buon volonta."*

During the evening Mrs. Cohen fingered each of the images tenderly, then asked, "What does the banner say, Mrs. Buscaglia?"

"Pace. Peace," Mama answered.

"Yes," Rabbi Cohen sighed. "Peace."

I can remember much laughter that night, but I recall more vividly the tears brought on by shared memories of "the old country." How much they missed the families left behind, the dear friends, the special foods now unavailable, the places of their childhood that perhaps they would never see again.

Several evenings later we sat in the Cohens' living room eating potato *latkes,* sharing small glasses of wine,

and breaking bread—the challah. We watched in silence as Mrs. Cohen lit the last of the Hanukkah candles from the flame of the *shammash*—eight in all—until the menorah was ablaze with light. Mrs. Cohen looked beautiful in the bright candlelight. "Like a Madonna," my mother told her. "Oy vey," Mrs. Cohen said, "a Jewish Madonna!" We listened to the prayers and the songs. Rabbi Cohen had a beautiful basso voice that towered over the others in a strange harmony. We were all presented with Hanukkah gifts. We learned to spin the dreidel, a great game that produced much laughter.

When the time came for us to depart, Rabbi Cohen put his arm around my father's shoulder. "Hanukkah isn't Christmas, but like your Christmas, it's a time of a miracle, a Festival of Light," he explained. He told us it celebrates a rededication of their temple, a reminder to put away thoughts of revenge and battle and share love in peace with family and friends. "Just like it says on your manger—time for 'Peace on earth to men of goodwill.'"

I can still visualize the moment when we departed from the Hanukkah celebration. Papa huddled us all together under umbrellas at the bottom of the Cohens' front porch. He turned and said, "Happy Hanukkah, *cari amici*." Rabbi Cohen, his family surrounding him, smiled

down at us, "Merry Christmas, neighbors. *Mazel tov!*"

This was the beginning of a loving friendship between our two families that was to last more than thirty years. Thirty years in which so many things happened, none of which we could foretell during that first special season. Rabbi Cohen died one day on his way to shul. His heart simply stopped. My brothers and sisters, one by one, left home. Elijah got married and I was his best man. His sister went off to college to become a doctor. Mrs. Cohen went to live with her brother in New York. My parents sold the family home and moved into a small apartment nearer to my elder sister.

Beautiful memories recalled have a way of re-creating the original glow and warmth surrounding them. I feel them still, writing these thoughts, even after fifty years. I can settle back and yield to the feeling of love we radiated during that holiday, a love that will never die as long as there is one of us to remember.

"Happy Hanukkah, *cari amici.*"

"Merry Christmas, neighbor. *Mazel tov!*"

A GIFT
OF
RAVIOLI

*There is no lesser or greater gift
if the gift is love.*

When I was a child I had a crush on a librarian. Once a week she held a story hour in the garden of our neighborhood library. She read to us wonderful tales of adventure, fantasy, and beauty. I was never absent from these sessions. In fact, I would often arrive hours early to assure myself a seat in the front row so as not to miss a single word.

I remember vividly the Christmas when she read Henry Van Dyke's *The Story of the Other Wise Man*. I was only eight or nine years old. Usually she read many stories in the allotted hour, but on this occasion she read only one.

After the reading was over she hugged us all a Merry Christmas. She took me by the hand and walked me outside, through the library. She knelt down beside me and smiled. "I've got a Christmas present for you. I want to give you the book I've just read." She handed me her copy of *The Story of the Other Wise Man*. "Did you enjoy the story?" she asked.

Frankly, I really didn't understand it, but of course I was not going to tell her that. Instead I said, "Yes, it was really interesting." In actuality, the story had confused

me. I couldn't imagine that anyone would be so insane as to give up, for any reason, being present in Bethlehem for the birth of Jesus of Nazareth. Nor could I understand that a person would give rubies and pearls, intended for Christ's birthday present to cruel soldiers and conniving debt collectors!

I recall that I went straight home clutching the little book in my hand, determined to read it once more. Surely if my wonderful friend loved the book, I would too.

As many know, the story tells of the magical voyage of the three Wise Men of the East, how they traveled from afar, guided by a single star, to bear gifts to a newborn King who was lying in a manger in Bethlehem. But it suggests that there was a fourth Wise Man, of whom I'd never heard, who also saw a star in the East and set off on the long, arduous journey to join the other Wise Men, bearing his precious gifts.

According to the story, the three Wise Men had no trouble getting to Bethlehem, but the fourth, Artaban, had nothing but problems. First he meets a sick Hebrew exile, alone and dying in the desert. Overcome with pity, he stops and ministers to the sick man. This delay causes him to miss his rendezvous with the other Wise Men,

and as a result he misses being present in the manger on that magical first Christmas.

Still, he travels on. Not long afterward he gives away one of the gifts intended for the newborn Child in order to save the life of another infant who, by Herod's decree, had been condemned to die. Time after time he stops to minister to the sick, comfort the oppressed and imprisoned, and feed the hungry.

As the story ends, Artaban is despairing and very tired. He realizes that he has been on his search for thirty-three years, ending by finding himself in Golgotha. Here he discovers that the Son of God, whom he had so many years ago set out to find, has been condemned to die on the cross. He immediately thinks of his very last possession, a pearl. He feels certain that this will buy Christ's freedom. But even on his way to try to bargain for Christ's life, he encounters a woman who is being threatened with assault and murder in payment for her father's debt. Again, he offers the pearl, his final possession, as ransom for her life.

Now he truly has nothing. All that he had intended to give in worship he has given in the service of humanity. To add to his trials, Artaban is struck by a stone from a falling structure, caused by the earthquake that accompanied the crucifixion. He is certain now that he will die

without ever seeing his Lord. But as he lies bleeding and dying he hears a faint voice from far off, "Verily, I say unto thee, inasmuch as thou hast done unto one of the least of my brethren, thou hast done unto Me." Hearing this, Artaban, the fourth Wise Man, dies with the happy knowledge that his gifts *were* received by his Lord.

At last I understood. While at first I had thought the Wise Man to be not so wise at all for missing his chance to witness the first Christmas, for giving away all his possessions, for having spent his entire life ministering to others, it all became clear to me. Artaban was certainly the wisest and most worthy of all the Wise Men.

I couldn't wait to tell the story to Mama and Papa. They had brought with them a tradition of storytelling and listened intently. When I finished they looked at each other for some time in silence. Then Mama spoke. "That's a nice story, Felice," she said. "And it's-a true. When you give what you have to help someone else, it's-a like giving to God."

Papa asked, "What you gonna give the nice library lady?"

Gee, I thought, *I don't have anything to give her.*

"I know," Mama said, "I'll make her a nice-a dish of ravioli."

"Ravioli!" I shouted. I was certain my precious friend,

who had just presented me with such a sophisticated gift, would scoff at Mama's ravioli. I wanted to give her rubies, frankincense, or *at least* myrrh (whatever that was!).

As usual, my protestations carried little weight and I was soon on my way to the library with a dish full of handmade ravioli and a jar of rich red sauce, both wrapped securely in brown paper bags. On the way I contemplated all the ways in which I could dispose of the gift. They would never know. I considered dropping it into a drain, throwing it behind the food market, or dumping it into a trash can. But conscience prevailed and propelled me into the library. There I discovered my love seated behind the checkout desk. "Leo," she greeted me warmly as I entered.

"I brought you a present," I explained, extending the bags at arm's length. "It's kinda dumb," I stammered. "It's something to eat for later."

She eagerly took the package and peered into the brown bag holding the ravioli dish. Her eyes lit up brightly.

"Ravioli!" she exclaimed. "Oh, I love ravioli. Thank you. It's not a dumb gift at all. It's a real treasure, more precious than jewels."

More precious than jewels? I thought.

Yes . . .

Of course . . .

I finally and truly understood *The Story of the Other Man.* Mama's ravioli took on a very special meanin

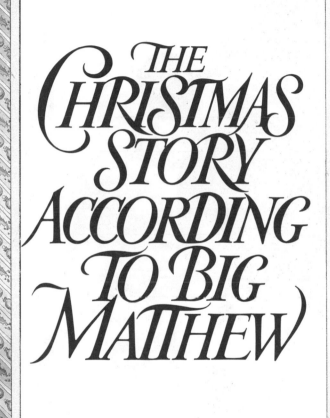

THE CHRISTMAS STORY ACCORDING TO BIG MATTHEW

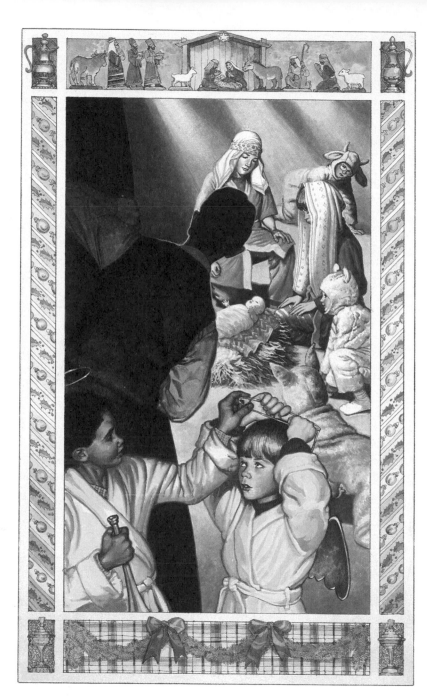

*If we ever forget
the meaning of Christmas,
all we need do
is listen to children.*

"Who would like to volunteer to take charge of the Christmas program?" the principal asked. There was a deadly silence. I had a feeling when I went to the faculty meeting that afternoon in November that the assignment as director of the Christmas Pageant would fall to me. I was right. I was the newest member of the staff, fresh out of the university, and having my first experience working with the seven- and eight-year-old second-graders who traditionally presented the program.

The pageant was to include Christmas songs and readings by the children, and culminate in the reenactment of the Christmas story and the celebration of Hanukkah. (Mrs. Klein always did the Hanukkah presentation, I was told, so there was never a problem with that.) The principal gave me the names of Mrs. Sagonski and Mrs. Zigretti, both active members of the PTA who would help me with the costumes. A Mr. Lambretta would be responsible for the sets.

For weeks prior to the scheduled date of the program the school was alive with sounds of "Jingle Bells," "Deck the Halls," "We Three Kings," and "Silent Night." The music teacher, Mrs. Chancellor, looked frantic as she

rushed from room to room with her Autoharps and her pitch whistle.

My classroom was a disaster area. I had decided that we would do a pantomime of the Christmas story, with narration and minimal dialogue. I was determined that no child in my class of thirty-two students would be excluded. I would find a role for everyone. We would have sheep, cows, goats, and even horses, if necessary, in the manger scene. I would have a multitude of angels, shepherds, the Three Wise Men, and, of course, Mary and Joseph.

Since I felt that the main thing the children should gain from the experience was the spirit of Christmas—the glory, the warmth, the simplicity, the beauty, and the mystery—I would start by reading to them the lovely biblical references to the birth of Christ. "And it came to pass in those days that there went out a decree from Caesar Augustus, that the world would be taxed." I read about Joseph, and Mary "being great with child," and how they went to Bethlehem, how when they arrived there was no room at the inn so Mary gave birth to her child, "wrapped him in swaddling clothes and laid him in a manger."

I read about the shepherds who were "keeping watch over their flock by night," and how the angel of the Lord

came to them and they were "sore afraid." I read how the angel told them not to fear but rather to rejoice, because born to them this day in the City of David was their savior, "which is Christ the Lord." And I told how the angels came in great numbers and proclaimed, "Glory to God in the highest and on earth, peace, good-will toward men."

I also read the beautiful description of the Three Wise Men, how they had seen the bright star in the eastern sky and had come so many miles to worship "the King of the Jews," carrying with them "gifts of gold, frankincense and myrrh."

The discussions that ensued were exciting, as only talking with seven- and eight-year-olds can be. They needed to know more about Caesar Augustus, decrees, "being great with child," swaddling clothes, "sore afraid," men from the East, and, of course, frankincense and myrrh. I learned a great deal with them that year.

Our curriculum supervisor, a rather tense woman in her fifties, advised me that I should prepare a script and have the children memorize it. In this way, she assured me, there would be no mishaps and we would not lose the beauty of the biblical language. As with all budding young professionals, I was not about to be told how to

teach my students. I decided instead that only the children's natural dialogue would do—anything less from their innocent lips would take away from the beauty and naturalness that only children can project. I was certain that if we practiced long enough with the biblical language, it might be altered here and there by the children, but perhaps sound even more natural and lovely.

I decided that it would be best for the class to choose among the students for the speaking roles rather than to have me assign them. For Mary they selected a very silent but lovely little girl whose name was Sarah. Some of the class wanted Sandra to play the part because she was the most talkative. But they were overruled. They felt that Mary would be more shy. Sandra had enough going for her in the class anyway, they agreed.

There was no argument about who should play Joseph. It was to be Big Matthew. Matthew was the tallest in the class and the strongest. He was also the most hyperactive. He never really sat in a chair; he seemed to hover precariously above it. Reading and arithmetic were a mystery for Matthew, but when he went out to recess or games he never failed to awe. He was modest about his athletic prowess and did much to encourage the less coordinated of our class, including myself. "That's OK,

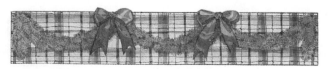

Mr. Buscaglia, you'll hit the ball someday!" The students were sure that he would be the perfect Joseph. I had my doubts.

We selected angels, shepherds, and the Three Wise Men. It seemed to me to be a cast of thousands. I soon began to understand the problems that Cecil B. De Mille must have had.

Mrs. Zigretti and Mrs. Sagonski were each a joy. They came into the classroom with the vitality of two tornadoes and started making the costumes with unrestrained gusto. It was amazing to watch how beautifully they handled the children. They cut and pinned and stitched the worn sheets and pieces of cloth they had gathered to clothe Mary and Joseph, the shepherds, the Wise Men, and the angels. The animals were another thing. How to create the illusion of cows, sheep, and pigs? Mrs. Sagonski advised that we give up the animals and make them all angels. "Angels are easy," she assured me. But it was Mrs. Zigretti who came to the rescue. "Who ever heard of a manger with no animals, and so full of angels?" In no way would she give up the project. Though the finished product was questionable, and some of the children couldn't tell a sheep from a goat from a cow, the children's faces peeking through the mounds of torn and wrapped materials were irresistible.

Mr. Lambretta's set design proved very simple. He used the dark-brown curtains already on the stage and put two stuffed flour sacks at center stage as seats for Mary and Joseph. He rationalized that there could not have been time for a cradle and they certainly would not be traveling with one. He assured me that under dark-blue floodlights a multitude of sins could easily be hidden. After all, theater was "illusion." Where Mr. Lambretta, an excellent plumber, got that information amazed me.

We rehearsed long and hard for many weeks. We learned entrances, exits, cues, and lines. The lines, being extemporaneous, were always a bit different, but tended to adhere to the written text. In fact, the main angel, a rather large and pretty child named Susie, learned her lines to perfection. She set a wonderful example and the others followed, learning their lines by rote as well.

I proceeded with the rehearsals as if we were preparing a Broadway production using the Stanislavski method of acting. We discussed "feelings": How about Mary and Joseph's love for one another and for their child? We analyzed reactions: What would shepherds look like if they were "sore afraid"?

After the chaos of the first rehearsals, things became much smoother. The major problems were getting shy

Sarah to speak loudly enough to be heard in the large, acoustically terrible auditorium; getting Matthew to stop bouncing around as if he had a toad in his pants pocket or was the next one up to bat; getting the animals to moo, baa, and oink on cue; and helping the Wise Men to maintain balance as they walked up the stairs to the stage bearing their gifts. I was certain that one of the three would surely end up in the orchestra pit.

Finally came the afternoon of the performance. The parents were assigned the last seven rows of the auditorium. We were all delighted that the seats were fully occupied. The supervisor and principal were in the front row. The classes all filed in and sat in their assigned sections. Backstage, I was trying unsuccessfully to keep the children quiet enough so that the audience could hear the principal, who had now risen and was welcoming the parents and students to the annual Christmas Pageant. This was followed by the tra-la-la-la-la of some carolers; then each classroom did a different holiday number under the guidance of Mrs. Chancellor, who was frantic but forcing a peaceful smile. I noticed from backstage that her eyes were pleadingly directed to the many children in the audience who couldn't seem to keep quiet; she winced from time to time like someone being lashed as punishment.

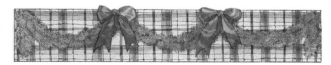

Mrs. Klein and her class, cool and relaxed, presented the Hanukkah ceremony. It went without a hitch. It was moving, beautiful, and perfectly executed, a model of good classroom planning and teaching.

Finally we got our cue from the chorus, who took off on "Silent Night." Mr. Lambretta plunged the stage into blue light. I hustled the children to their places. The final lines of the Christmas carol were sung—"Christ the Savior is bo-o-o-orn, Christ the Savior is born."

At this moment, the curtain opened, disclosing Mary and Joseph leaning against each other, seated on their flour sacks and peacefully sleeping. They were surrounded by the cherubic animals uttering their pastoral sounds. Cynthia forgot she was a sheep and was mooing like her girlfriend Roberta. Raul Gonzales, one of the sheep, and certainly the most shy child in the class, took one look at the vast audience, headed for the wings, and disappeared. This seemed to faze no one but me. The children were too busy being sheep, cows, and pigs. On cue, the number-one angel appeared. Her wings were drooping and looked as if they might fall off at any moment, but she remained poised and undaunted. In her arms she carried the baby Jesus. She placed the child carefully on the straw at Mary's feet, then faced the audience, and in round, pear-shaped tones she announced,

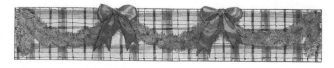

"And it came to pass . . ." She got as far as Caesar Augustus before she faltered, but picked up again and went bravely on, ". . . wrapped him in swaddling clothes and laid him in a manger."

At this point, Matthew awakened. He yawned and looked down in surprise, discovering the child at Mary's feet. To this day I cannot imagine what possessed him. Perhaps it was my teaching him the Stanislavski method. In the past the scene had always been performed in quiet gestures of love and wondrous delight. On this occasion he shook Mary's shoulder rather roughly. "Mary! Mary!" he shouted. "Wake up and see what you had during the night!"

I heard several gasps from the audience. One of the fathers present broke up with laughter and even spontaneously applauded.

The pageant continued, though I was never again fully aware of what was happening. *(Matthew! What have you done to me?)* The shepherds, I am told, were very "sorely afraid." No Wise Men ended up in the orchestra pit. And even Raul was persuaded to go back onto the stage. All's well, I felt, that ends well.

When the program ended, the children excitedly scampered out of their costumes, ready for their two-week holiday. The parents gathered on the stage, collected their

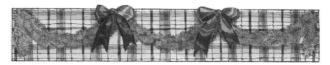

children, congratulated me, and disappeared in the wave of excitement.

It was then that the principal appeared. "Mr. Buscaglia," she said, "when you're through here, I'd like to see you in my office." Just at that moment, the father who had been so enthusiastic about Big Matthew's statement rushed forward. "The best darn Christmas Pageant I've ever seen," he said. "Children say the darndest things! 'See what you had during the night!'" he repeated. "That's rich!" The principal looked at us for a moment, then left the stage. I was certain that my teaching career had just been brought to an abrupt end. The supervisor had been right—I should have played it safe rather than try for magic.

I was admitted immediately into the principal's office. She looked larger than ever behind her desk. As I entered, a smile formed on her lips. "It was beautiful!" she said. "The children were wonderful and so were you to have taken on this job. I've never had so much fun. And I've never known the simplicity and wonder of the Christmas story to be captured better. And wasn't Matthew a jewel!"

She rose from her desk and came toward me in genuine warmth. "You're doing a great job, Leo. You'll make a truly exceptional teacher one day." I stammered

a hesitant thank you and started out of the office. "Have a nice, quiet, and restful holiday," she called after me, "and a wonderful Christmas."

Before I left the school I met Matthew in the hall. He told me he had decided not to be a baseball player when he grew up. Now he wanted to become an actor! "I guess I'll have to learn how to read then, won't I?" he added.

"Yes, Matthew," I said, putting my hand on his sandy-haired head. "And have a very merry Christmas!"

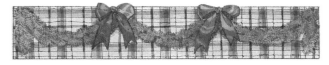

A SANTA SUIT DOES NOT A SANTA CLAUS MAKE

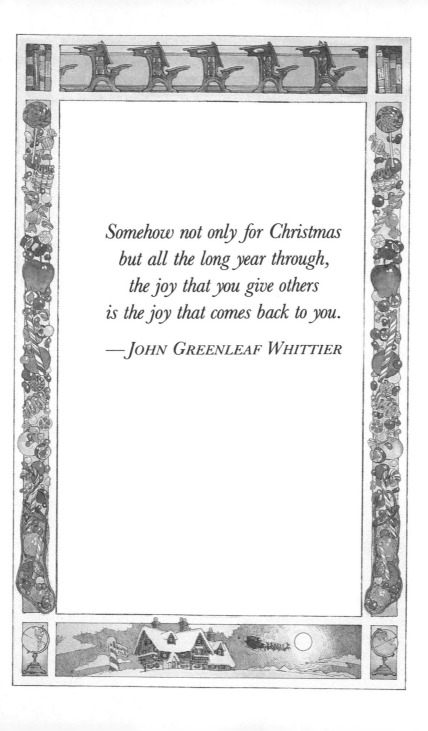

Somehow not only for Christmas
but all the long year through,
the joy that you give others
is the joy that comes back to you.

—JOHN GREENLEAF WHITTIER

*E*ach time the pressures of a Christmas season begin to get to me, and one more piped-in carol assaults my ears in yet another crowded shopping mall, I think of a Christmas so many years ago when I was a very young teacher. The school was alive with activity as we prepared for the special days to come. There was much to do. We had to decorate our classrooms, rehearse our parts in the Christmas play, plan the trip to sing in a local retirement home, and, of course, make the much-anticipated gifts for Mom and Dad.

One day prior to the holiday break, I was called to the principal's office. Our usually calm and collected principal seemed to be in a state of high anxiety. "We've lost our Santa Claus!" she moaned. "Mr. Ruggles is usually our Santa, but he is ill. A very bad cold, maybe even pneumonia."

I couldn't imagine Mr. Ruggles, the school custodian, being ill. He was a large, jovial man with a bright, sunny face and rosy cheeks that would be the envy of any Santa Claus.

I was beginning to recover from the news when I heard the principal suggest that since I was the only

other man in the school (male teachers in elementary schools were rare at that time), I was the logical replacement. She explained that she herself had considered replacing him, but a woman Santa just wouldn't do.

"I know you'll do it," she said. "You would never disappoint the children."

The idea sounded like madness to me. In the first place, I was so thin at the time that I was compelled to buy my clothes in children's sizes. And though I could manage a booming voice when necessary, I knew I wasn't up to the traditional "Ho, ho, ho!"—so important to an authentic Santa Claus.

"But I don't look anything like Santa Claus. The kids will see it in a minute and laugh me out of the room," I protested.

"Nonsense," she assured me, "you'll make a magnificent Santa. It's nothing. All you have to do is visit each classroom with the bag of toys. When you see the children, greet them and be merry, pass out candy canes, then make a fast exit to your next room. I'll carry the bells."

"But . . ." I tried to interject, though I could see that it was useless. She was already dragging me into her office, where she had a large Santa outfit draped across her desk.

"Now get into this quickly," she said.

"But what about my classroom?" I made one last effort.

"Never mind. We'll get it covered."

"But I'll make a miserable Santa."

"Well, even a miserable Santa will be better than none at all," she replied, and left me to change clothes.

In a few minutes she was back, stuffing pillows inside the Santa suit, fitting the cap on my head over the white wig, gluing on the beard and painting bright rosy cheeks and lips on my face. When she was finished, I looked in the mirror and was pleasantly surprised to discover that I actually made a respectable-looking Santa.

"Come on, now," the principal encouraged me. "Let's have a big Christmas smile!" I found that a little difficult to accomplish, but I managed a little grin.

I tightened the black belt around my billowing pillows and followed her jingling bells out into the hall. "We'll go to the kindergarten first," she told me as we approached Room 1.

The response to my entrance was deafening. Sounds of clapping hands and screams of delight filled the room. With glowing eyes and grasping hands, the children surrounded me, attaching themselves to my spindly legs and

very nearly pulling my oversized pants down around my ankles.

"Ho, ho, ho," I heard myself say, not being able to think of anything more creative. "Have you all been good boys and girls?"

"Y-E-E-E-E-S!" came the joyous response.

"Not John," said one of the more poised girls, in a rather motherly tone of voice. "He hasn't been good, has he, teacher?"

"Well," stammered the teacher, rather stunned, "he's trying."

"I have candy for everyone," I said. In an instant I was downed like a quarterback in a failed play, inundated with tiny bodies bursting with anticipation.

With a firm voice, the teacher saved me from suffocation. I quickly regained my lost dignity and took the occasion to hand out the candy canes to the eager extended hands. I had never seen such happy faces, such unaffected joy. It didn't matter to them that by this time I had become totally unglued, my moustache hanging precariously over my lips, my gigantic stomach sliding down over my legs. None of these things mattered to the children. I was Santa Claus, and that was all that had any real importance. This joy-filled spirit was evident in each

classroom, no matter the children's ages.

Though I had felt awkward and tentative at the start, I was soon caught up in the wonder of what was happening. I found myself behaving like the kind old man himself, the giver of good things, the renewer of hope, the dispenser of magic. For a while I was certain that I could actually make dreams into realities, turn the mundane into wonder.

For the first time I realized how powerful the symbol of Santa is. With a "Ho, ho, ho" he has the power to paint a drab classroom the color of sunshine, and turn an often cheerless school into a wonderland.

When I returned to the principal's office fifteen classrooms later, I was in a pretty ragged state. I removed my costume and makeup. The principal and teachers streamed in and out to offer congratulations on my stunning performance and to assure me that I had saved Christmas.

Most of the cars were gone when I went to the school parking lot later that afternoon. I had left Santa Claus where I had found him, draped over the principal's desk. As I was about to open the door of my car I saw one of the children coming toward me, devouring the candy cane Santa had given him.

"How did you like Santa Claus?" I asked him.

"Oh," he answered, "you were great, Mr. B."

I was stunned.

So the children had recognized me all along, yet it hadn't mattered. They hadn't expected the real Santa Claus; any symbol was fine with them—even a rather ragged, skinny one.

Now during the Christmas season, when I find myself trying to deal with the pressures of the time and all the trappings of a commercialized Christmas, I stop and recall what the children taught me on that special day. It isn't the Santa suit that makes the Santa, any more than it is the tinsel, colored lights, and sounds of cash registers that make Christmas. Then, like a child, I gather my gifts and, savoring a candy cane, I start for home, renewed and ready for the celebration and true wonder that is uniquely Christmas.

NO ROOM AT THE INN

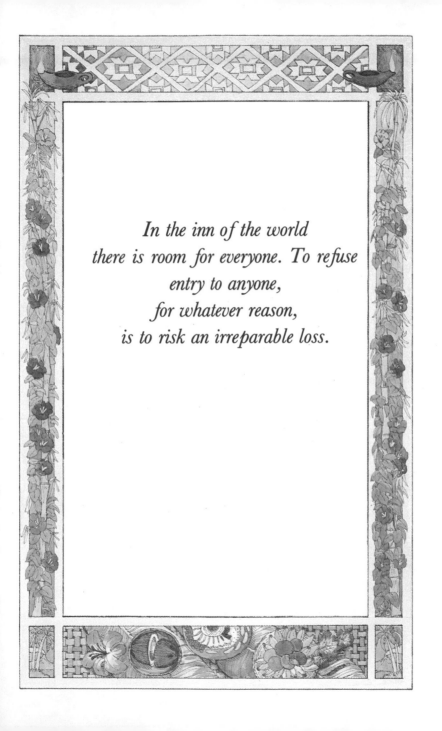

*In the inn of the world
there is room for everyone. To refuse
entry to anyone,
for whatever reason,
is to risk an irreparable loss.*

I arrived in Bali on the day before Christmas. The bus driver, with a broad betel nut–stained smile, stopped at a fork in the road. He pointed down a narrow paved street. Like most roads in Bali, it cut straight into the dense jungle only to vanish in heat mist. "Ubud," he said.

I thanked him, shook his hand, waved good-bye to my fellow passengers, and waited as he started the small rickety bus with a loud blast and disappeared down the main road.

The morning was still relatively cool. December was a good month for Bali, with hot days, balmy nights, and long afternoons ending in spectacular multicolored sunsets.

From what I had been told in Denpasar, the palace of the Agung was less than an hour's walk down the road. In Asia, distance is measured by time.

I took a firm grip on my suitcase and started out. Brown-skinned Balinese draped in gorgeous batik began to appear from nowhere, carrying bundles of fresh fruit, bottles of colored liquids, animals in various stages of approaching death, and plump, smiling naked infants.

The almond-eyed, bare-breasted young girls moved quickly like ballerinas, while handsome hard-bodied boys, whose skin glistened like deeply waxed mahogany, ran and chattered together.

Occasional dirt paths cut their way into the jungle from the narrow road, suggesting the location of settlements here and there in the brush. Small wooden shacks, partially hidden between bushes on the banks, hung precariously over the road. Crooked stone steps rose to doors that stood open, welcoming the cool early-morning air.

Houses became more frequent, more people appeared, and soon I approached the center square of Ubud. There, towering over everything in pink beauty, was the wall of the palace compound, facing what seemed to be a large open-air assembly area. On the opposite side of the road were several small shops selling wood carvings and the famous paintings of Bali.

The Agung had received a letter from one of his hundreds of relatives throughout the islands of Indonesia and was expecting me. He was a rather jolly rotund man, dark-skinned, with a friendly smile, whose favorite expression, learned while attending school in England, was unexpectedly "Gee, goodness me!"

"Gee, goodness me," he greeted me, "I knew you were

coming, but I did not know exactly when. Welcome."

Two little boys ran out and attached themselves to his fat legs below the drape of his knee-length sarong. "These are my sons," he said proudly, "and those playing there are also my children. And gee, goodness me, those women on the veranda are my wives. You will meet them tonight. Tonight we talk."

There was a moment of silence as he detached his children gently from his legs and lifted them affectionately into his arms. "Ratab," he called. "Ratab is my servant." Ratab appeared dressed in Western-style clothes, all in white. His face was round, dark, alive, with dancing eyes, a broad smile, and even, white teeth. Ratab stood staring at me while the Agung continued, "Will you stay here on the palace grounds, or will you take one of the cottages on the hill near the river?" He did not wait for my answer, but continued, "I have many interesting guests now—an American schoolteacher on vacation from Sumatra, an Irish painter who came for a week and has been here for seven years, and a very important person from the consulate in Djakarta. There is still room in the palace. There is no one in the cottages."

"I think I'd like a cottage if it means no additional trouble."

"Gee, goodness me, no. Ratab will be there with you to

take care of what you may need. It will be good for him, too. It will give him a chance to practice his English. We will send a servant ahead to get the place ready and Ratab will show you how to get there. It is not too far."

As we started out of the court, he called, "Gee, goodness me, come to dinner at seven."

We reached the road and started up the slow incline that led to the cottages. Ratab explained that he was seventeen years old, had a secondary-school education, and was now studying English in Denpasar. He was neither shy nor aggressive, but had a simple, honest quality that was most charming. "You will like the cottages," he said. "I'm happy that you chose to stay there. There are many flowers and birds, and all is green. You get no dust from the road, and at night, when all is quiet, you can hear the song of the river. I stay there only when we have a guest. I am happy that you chose the cottage."

"It's beautiful here," I said. "It's a perfect place to spend Christmas."

"Christmas?" he asked. "What is Christmas?" This was unexpected. I had forgotten that there were many in the world who had never heard of Christianity.

"Christmas is the birthday of the Christian God, Jesus."

Ratab was perhaps the most curious individual I have

met in all my travels. Not simply a childlike curiosity but a deep interest obsessed him that was not satisfied until he understood exactly, with no question, what was implied or stated. He would never allow a question in his mind to remain unanswered.

"Who is the Christian God, Jesus?" he asked.

"Like your God, Vishnu. Well, sort of."

So I started a rather simple telling of the Christmas story. Until this time, as often as I had heard the story, I had never realized what an exciting, charming, and delightfully mystical tale it is. As I spoke, we walked through a dense rain forest of lush ferns, tall tropical trees and shrubs that easily dwarfed us, and flowers that hung everywhere in splashes of orange, yellow, pink, and red, all entwined in the deep green of the landscape.

"I hear the river!" I interrupted my tale.

"Yes," Ratab answered. "It flows beneath the rope bridge ahead. But why would not the people allow Mary and Joseph to share their bed?"

I explained that neither Mary nor Joseph knew anyone in Bethlehem. This did not seem to make any difference to Ratab, who insisted that someone should have made room for them in their bed.

"But they did not know that Mary was to give birth to their God, Jesus."

"That is not important," Ratab insisted matter-of-factly. "If Mary was traveling, if she was going to have a child, what matter if it were a god or not? They should have given her a place to rest." There was certainly no arguing with this statement and I realized that there were some things I would never be able to explain to Ratab.

I changed the subject, telling him about the significance of the Christmas tree. He was delighted with the idea and the giving of gifts, and laughed at the thought of a "jolly old Santa Claus," though I was not quite able to explain the connection between Santa Claus and the God, Jesus, to his satisfaction. "Why does not Santa Claus dress as Jesus?" he asked.

In a few moments we had come to a steep gorge, green and rich with color. At the bottom rushed a clear river, purring its way over and around rocks of odd shapes and sizes.

"This is our river," Ratab said. "It is a most sacred river because all our ancestors are buried here, and their remains flow in the stream. We bathe here each day. You must bathe with us."

We crossed over the shaky rope bridge. Below were groups of naked people, splashing happily in the river, washing their sarongs or drying their bodies in the warm sun.

"Tell me of the snow in Bethlehem," Ratab said suddenly. "Of what use is snow? And then you must explain why they would not let Mary and Joseph stay at the inn."

After crossing the bridge, we made a sharp turn to our right and down a steep stairway. There, in a natural garden of grass and flowers, stood four square thatch-roofed cottages.

"You must take the top cottage," Ratab told me. "From it you can see the mountains, the river, the valley, and the sky."

Each cottage had a large living area covered with palm branches and open to the jungle. The bedroom was half as large, with wall-length pull-up shutters and a small Western-style bed. The bathroom had a cesspool and a stone sink into which fresh water was poured daily for washing. The water was carried up from the river. All around the rooms were small oil lamps made of clay. The hard dirt floor was swept clean.

It was now shortly after noon. The sun was hot, but pleasant. Ratab went off for a while to send the houseboy for food. The Christmas story had made a great impression on him. He accepted it without question except for the fact of Mary being denied lodging. "Certainly, two

persons do not take very much space. It is very strange, indeed."

I looked out into the afternoon. The sun's rays pierced through leaves and flowers like an X ray, each one a unique, intricate design and color.

When Ratab returned he was followed by a tall, thin young man with shy and downcast eyes. His brown body was partially covered with a fading batik loin cloth. His long legs were straight and muscular. He carried a tray covered with small dishes of exotic foods, which he set before me. Then he left without a word.

Ratab sat beside me and explained each dish as I ate the subtle-tasting savory mixtures. Now and again one could hear the sound of footsteps and laughter as the natives walked down the cliff on their way to the river. Some paused to look at us, seemingly delighted that one of the cottages was again occupied.

When I finished eating, Ratab said, "Now you must rest. Later, I will take you to bathe. If you want anything, call Adja. He will be here with you all the time, night and day." He had no sooner said this than Adja appeared to remove the tray. He did not raise his eyes as we were introduced.

I removed my clothes and climbed into bed. From a

reclining position I could see the tops of the tall palms, some orange and purple bougainvillea, the fluffy edge of a white cloud, and the blue sky. As the heat became more intense, the afternoon awakened all at once with the myriad sounds of life in Bali: the buzz of the insects, the murmur and splash of the river, soft footsteps, voices and laughter. Adja entered silently and lowered the shutters. I fell asleep instantly.

It was late afternoon when Ratab awakened me. It was still hot and my sheets were wet with perspiration. "It is time to bathe," he said. He carried a patterned batik, which he helped me tie around my body.

The path down the cliff to the river was wide enough for only one person to move along—with caution. It was patted firm by the many hard-soled bare feet that mounted and descended each day. Ferns and flowers bordered it, hanging gently just out of reach.

What before had been the constant sibilant sound of the river now became a roar as we descended into the gorge. From above, the river had seemed narrow and gracefully bouncy, but at close view it revealed its rushing strength. In some places the water was clear enough for us to discern the stony bottom; in others the river floor vanished in foam and deep color. Clever damming created the bathing areas. A group of men in various

bathing postures, tanned and hardened by the sun and streaked with soap foam, greeted us as we reached the river. Ratab pointed to a clear spot on a large rock. "Here," he said. We stripped and under the curious eyes of the other bathers plunged into the cold water. The initial shock brought the usual reaction, causing the others to laugh, relax, and then resume what they were doing before our arrival.

When we had soaped and bathed and were lying in the sun to dry, the group assembled about Ratab with expressions that seemed to ask, "Well, who is this strange white man?" Ratab explained with understandable gestures that I was staying in the cottage on the hill as the guest of the Agung, and that I was from far-off America. One by one they glanced sideways at me, my smile meeting theirs in a language of its own.

Through Ratab we all learned a few simple facts about each other: I was a professor from America, one was a painter, another made wood carvings, others worked their fathers' rice fields, and so on. As our initial strangeness wore off, we each found our own language to tell our story.

"House." "Your." "There."

"Water." "Cold." "Nice."

"This rock better, smoother."

"Sun warmer here."

"Come, lie with us here."

Soon I was surrounded by naked, shining bodies, by lips murmuring in a strange, wondrous language, and by smiles rivaling each other for warmth and beauty.

Calmly Ratab began to talk. He was obviously telling them something that meant a great deal to him. The group was intent on every word. I found myself listening along with the others. Every now and then I seemed to hear "Jesus," "Mary," "Bethlehem," and it became clear that he was telling them the Christmas story. I lay back and closed my eyes, lulled by the sounds of the lilting language.

We all left the river together, walking up the path directly toward the setting sun. As it dropped behind the trees it seemed to cling to the palm leaves, then reluctantly release them and dip out of sight behind the rain forest, leaving the sky a hundred colors. I said good-bye to the group at my cottage door and stood listening to their laughter and watching them as they scaled the last small incline and vanished into the sunset. Ratab said he would return in a few hours to escort me to the palace for dinner.

As I dressed that evening I seemed to hear a soft moan, or was it a strange weeping? I walked out into the

dusk. The cry seemed to be coming from the dense rain forest across the river where there was certainly no human habitation. At first I felt sure that it must be the breeze that had suddenly come up, but then it sounded too human, too desperate. Night came suddenly with a deep purpleness which covered everything. Only then did I realize that the oil lamps in the cottage were lit. I had neither seen nor heard Adja, though obviously he was very much present. Entering the bedroom I found him lighting another small lamp.

The weeping sound seemed even louder now. I took Adja by the arm and pointed toward the sound in the blackness. He did not immediately understand, but after a moment he nodded. Then for the first time he spoke. His voice was at once excited and animated. Of course, I understood nothing. Upon finishing his complicated explanation, which he assumed I could understand, he took me into the bathroom and showed me the clear water he had carried from the river for my shave.

Ratab arrived shortly, dressed in a richly colored sarong. His dark hair was partly hidden under a small two-cornered hat of red silk. His chest was bare, broad, and smooth. He carried a small oil lamp to light our way to the palace. We crossed the footbridge in silence. The night noises were overpowering. The river's voice

sounded clear and constant although the river could not be seen. I wondered about the moan, which was no longer audible, but I did not want to disturb the night mood with my questions.

The Agung was silhouetted in the palace entrance when we arrived. He seemed younger.

"Gee, goodness me," he said. "You have come at last. It is the birthday of my youngest son. They are waiting for us." He took my arm and led me through the small dimly lit square and into a cluster of trees and flowers.

"Ratab told me that you related the Christmas story to him. Yes, it will be Christmas. I have ordered a Christmas dinner for you. You seem to have won over the young men of the village. You will find them very sincere and very good. I am happy that you want to know them."

We entered another court, typical of the inner courtyards in Balinese homes, surrounded by tall walls and containing several small structures—huts, a place of worship, and studios. In the rear of the compound was a small elevated stage. Informally seated about it were all of the Agung's children, twenty or more, and several beautiful women. On the platform were an old priest, a woman, and the birthday child.

The Agung mounted the platform, kissed the child,

and sat on a large chair. He insisted that I follow him and sit next to him in a place of honor. The ceremony was short and consisted mostly of sharing an odd-tasting drink and murmuring a short prayer. This was followed by much rejoicing on the part of the children and by the eating of wondrous sweets and savory fruits.

A large white sheet was then stretched across the platform, and after everyone had gathered before it, a puppeteer worked behind it, treating us to a fantastic shadow play. The story was simple and required only a word or two of explanation. The Agung was delighted that I was acquainted with their holy book, the *Ramayana*, as it was an episode of this epic that was being produced. For about fifteen minutes Rama battled the forces of evil with those of good, and the children watched as he succeeded. The puppeteer supplied all the voices and manipulated the various graceful, grotesque puppets with ease.

The Agung rose when the performance was over. "You must see the truly great stories done by the master." He smiled to the assembled group. A child ran to the Agung to be picked up and hugged to his bare shoulder. "Gee, goodness me," he said, handing the child to one of the women. "Let us go to dinner."

We walked back to the palace dining room, which was lit with oil lamps of great beauty. There, on a large

round table, were more than twenty dishes with a large suckling pig in the center. The odors were fantastic. Seated on cushions around the table were the other guests. The American schoolteacher was about thirty years old and wore Balinese dress. He was obviously trying hard to appear Indonesian. The Irish painter had a long, straggly beard, spoke with a brogue, and smiled deeply and calmly, as if he had achieved some secret insight from his seven years in Bali. Only the Indonesian dignitary from the consulate was in Western-style clothing and seemed strangely out of place in the group.

When the introductions were over I was seated on a pillow at the table and two graceful women silently began to serve us. The Agung cut the pig, taking great pains to see that each of us had his share of the crackling skin. Each dish was elegant—fish, vegetables, rice, fowl, fruit.

After dinner the group relaxed on their pillows and the conversation started. The Agung's participation revealed his facility with the English language, his keen wit, his clear mind, and his exciting ideas about life.

"Here in Bali things have not changed as in other parts of Indonesia. Somehow we continue to live as we please. It is true there is some hunger and poverty, but this is not a new condition among our people. We have

learned to live with nature. We are a people who love happiness. We need little—we dance, we play our music, we work. Art comes easily in Bali, for all is art and the search for beauty is not difficult. It is everywhere. Beauty is our way of life. If you say 'Growl not, stomach, there is nothing to put in thee' long enough, the stomach learns and growls less. In Ubud we are better off than most, for we are a colony of artists. My people are painters and dancers and wood carvers. Tourists come to look. We show them our beauty. We have changed our painting in some cases to suit their tastes. Therefore we have to some small extent compromised with the rest of the world. But compromise enables us to eat, sleep, and live as we please. We are a superstitious people. We are affectionate without being passionate. We are strong without forgetting how to be dependent. We are proud without losing sight of the strength in being humble. I hope," he said to me, "that you will stay long enough to know us."

The evening passed quickly. Ratab came out of the nowhere into which he had disappeared, carrying another oil lamp.

"Ah, how quickly time passes. It is time for us to go already," the Agung said as he rose and rubbed his round belly. "Merry Christmas to you all, and to all a good-night. Is that not Charles Dickens?" he laughed.

The night had become lighter. The sky was filled with stars. We returned to the cottage in silence. Ratab put his arm warmly about my shoulder and held the lamp before us. "It is a beautiful Christmas night," he said. When we reached the incline, Ratab preceded me down the side and helped me toward the cottage. In the doorway stood a banana tree that had been trimmed into the shape of a pine tree. On each branch were tied several flowers of assorted colors, and scattered about the tree were small clay oil lamps like tiny stars. "Your Christmas tree," he said simply.

I stood in the darkness before the tree. The lamp lights flickered slightly in the warm breeze. My eyes welled with tears. Ratab watched me closely. Assuming this was the tradition, he mustered tears and joined me in a good cry. After some time we entered the cottage. The room was crowded with some of the same boys I had bathed with and others I had not seen before. Each, Ratab indicated, had brought me a Christmas present—bananas, coconuts, papayas, pieces of batik, paintings, and even oil lamps of various shapes and sizes.

I sat on the floor among them and the conversation never stopped. They all wanted to hear the story of Christmas from me. With Ratab translating, no more flowery presentation was ever made. When the story was

told, I passed the fruit and, while they were eating, went into the bedroom. What did I have to give them? I had so little with me. I took everything from the suitcase that I could give away—my T-shirts, briefs, shirts, socks—no matter what, it was the spirit. They were all delighted with their gifts and discarded their elaborate batiks to put on jockey shorts and T-shirts, all too large for their slim bodies. They began to dance and sing and were pleased when I joined them.

In the midst of all the laughter, the sounds from across the river could again be heard. This time I felt sure the sound was a human weeping.

"What is that, Ratab?" I asked.

"Oh, it is the spirits," he said simply. "Bali has many spirits. The forest is full of them. They are everywhere. The spirit you hear is a very sad one. They say that he was Dutch and that he loved a girl from Ubud and was killed in the war. The girl leaped from this very cliff into the sacred river, so she too has never died. Do not have fear. Spirits who love do no harm. Bali is a land of spirits."

The festivity continued for a while and then Ratab announced that I must be tired and that it was time for sleep. Then he explained that several of the guests had asked for the honor of staying overnight.

"When you have made a new friend," he explained, "it is bad manners to leave him." The bed was small but Ratab picked six of the guests to join me. They put me in the middle and arranged their bodies about me. Like joyfully exhausted children, they fell asleep instantly— one holding my hand, another with his head on my shoulder, another with his leg over mine.

I stared up at the thatched roof and listened to the even breathing of my bed partners. The light of a single oil lamp danced about the room. Outside, the Christmas tree glittered beneath the stars.

Ratab, who had taken the place of honor at my side, slid his arm under my head. "I still don't understand why they could not make room for Mary." After a moment of silence he said, "Well, Merry Christmas," and fell asleep.

THE
CHRISTMAS
THAT
ALMOST
WASN'T

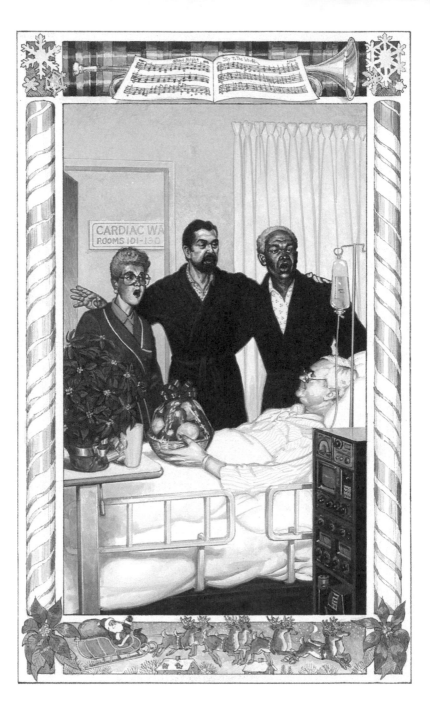

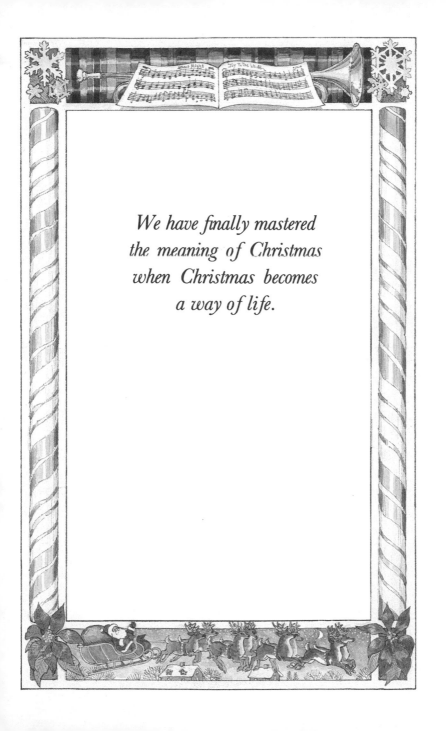

*We have finally mastered
the meaning of Christmas
when Christmas becomes
a way of life.*

here is no way I could suspect, as I drove to the hospital on that damp December morning, that it would be a one-way trip. Repeating ritualistically what I had done in previous years, I parked in the limited outpatient parking area and proceeded to the admissions office, where I filled out the necessary forms for my annual routine physical exam.

It was Christmastime, 1982. In the center of the waiting room was a magnificent Christmas tree. It was a welcome and glowing touch. Carols were being piped in via Muzak to keep us mindful of this special time of year, and to remind us that "'tis the season to be jolly," that "we'd better be good," that we should be decorating "the halls with boughs of holly" and generally preparing for the "holy night" to come.

I love the feel of holidays. They have always been eagerly anticipated family events for the Buscaglias. When Papa was dying he called my elder sister to his bedside and pleaded with her to take on the role of "keeping the family together." He was convinced, as was Mama before him, that the best way to do this was with frequent joint celebrations over food. "Rituals are good for the

mind and the heart," he'd say. "They give us something to look forward to, to count on. There can never be enough times for celebration."

My sister took this mandate so to heart that she and her husband built a huge family room which they were certain would last for generations of family gatherings. Holiday get-togethers for the family would be assured. In a few years it became apparent that only if we were to hire the grand ballroom of the local hotel could we house the entire family in one place, at one time. Families, especially Italian families, have a way of growing and getting out of hand. We were compelled to divide into two groups of revelers in two separate locations.

So it was on this Christmas—separate family celebrations, but together in love. The pasta was readied. The antipasto was planned, sliced, and marinated. The fowls were purchased and ready for stuffing. The Christmas breads and cookies were baked and the chestnuts boiled. Days ahead, both my sisters' kitchens were feasts for the senses: foods in tempting arrays of color, shape, texture, and size; the heavenly aromas of fresh rosemary, oregano, sage, onions, basil, and garlic. This was to be a banquet befitting the palates that Mama and Papa had spent years educating.

That I was not to partake of these wonders never

entered my mind. At the insistence of my doctor, I had saved Christmas break from university classes to take my annual physical examination. There I had a massive heart attack. Fortunately for me, it happened in the hospital. I fell into the arms of a cardiologist just a few feet away from the cardiac ward. It occurred quickly, without warning, and was totally incapacitating. Within hours it became apparent that if I were going to live, I would have to submit to emergency surgery—a quintuple bypass.

It is often said that Italians are among the most outwardly emotional people in the world. In fact, their longevity is often attributed to this tendency to express what is being felt inwardly, then, once expressed, let go. A case in point was my family's response to my illness. When the severity of my condition became known, the entire clan was plunged into hysteria and despair.

No way was there to be a Christmas celebration with me in the hospital. Never! Tears, prayers, rosaries, and mourning, yes, but merrymaking under such conditions was not to be even remotely considered. It was generally agreed that all holiday plans would be immediately canceled. There would be no Buscaglia Christmas.

It took most of my remaining energy to elicit a meager promise that the holiday would continue as planned,

without me. After all, I reasoned, everything was ready: the food (and they would have to eat), the meeting place (and they would want to be near family at such a time), the gifts—already purchased and wrapped and under the tree (and I would not want to be the cause of the children missing out on what they had been so long anticipating). I could not be certain that the family was entirely convinced, but they tearfully left my hospital room with a promise of sorts: They would get together for my sake, but they would not be happy about it.

Finally, alone in the silence of my room, I became acutely aware of the presence of Christmas. All the nurses were wearing corsages of holly and mistletoe. Decorated trees were giving off the scent of fresh pine. Carols blended softly with the routine hospital noises—"Silent night, holy night."

The monitors above my head, constantly recording my heart activity, continued to suggest the urgency of my condition and the awesome realization that this might well be my last Christmas.

It's a strange and inexplicable characteristic of human beings that we never seem to appreciate things until there is a possibility of having them taken from us. Small things that don't always rate our attention take on renewed meaning. We begin to see more clearly how we

sometimes lose ourselves in the mundane and the unimportant. We wonder how we found so many petty things to grumble about, or why we failed to stop long enough to experience the beauty of the season and the wonder of giving and celebrating.

I wondered, then, how we become desensitized to the special crispness in the air, the beauty of the holiday ornaments, the aroma of special foods, the excitement, the hugs, the laughter, and the kisses. It was very sobering to realize that by morning all these things might be taken from me—lost forever.

Thankfully, in spite of some minor complications, the operation was a success. The whole situation took on a sense of miracle. A surgeon whom I had met only briefly had, with a knowing touch, taken my heart into his hand, attached new arteries to it, and placed it carefully back in place—a rebirth of sorts. The wonder of it all.

I awoke in intensive care. It was like moving through a deep fog—aware, yet lost. I was a maze of tubes, bottles, pumps, and respirators. But even in my dazed state, I was aware that Christmas was everywhere. It brought a sense of relief. Wherever I was, it was Christmas there, too.

Within days I was moved into a private room in the cardiac ward. A constant parade of loved ones made

their way to my bedside. Each person was bearing gifts, things they were certain I couldn't live without: baked lasagna, homemade sausage, salami, mortadella, pureed chestnuts, cut flowers, potted plants, and my favorite holiday treat—*frittura dussa,* breaded cornmeal with lemon peel, fried in butter.

By week's end my room looked and smelled like nothing so much as the gala opening of an Italian deli. It wasn't like being at home, of course. I missed the children and the noise, but it was certainly the next best thing.

When visitors leave and darkness falls in a hospital, an eerie ambiance comes over the place. It was during one of these periods, while walking silently and cautiously around the ward, that I became aware of my neighbors. Seeing them alone, in semidarkness, I had the sudden inspiration to share my good fortune. To the elderly woman in the room immediately next to mine I gave my blooming poinsettia and a healthy serving of my sister's best egg custard. With the man down the hall who had (I'd been told) lost the will to live, I shared my largest array of cut flowers. I also delivered a portion of *frittura dussa,* which I was certain would add a new spark and perhaps an eagerness to try some more. The succulent wonder of that ambrosia is of itself reason enough to live.

In a few hours we all became fast friends, bound together by the same mystery of the shared moment. We decided to organize as charter members of the "Open Heart Club," class of '82. We formed a welcoming committee for the new patients who were steadily joining our ranks. We gave solace, encouragement, and love to them, their families, and their friends. We cried together. We laughed a lot. We had good reason for shared joy. Choice was still ours and, in the hospital or out, Christmas could still be what we wanted to make it. We had all been given the most precious gift of all—time for life.

I shall never forget that Christmas—which almost wasn't. Soon after that I returned home and shared two family Christmases, one in January and one in March.

I am more aware now than ever of my mortality. At some time, still unknown, I might not be as fortunate as I was in 1982. But it is useless to dwell on that. Rather, I will accept the challenge it suggests to make the rest of my life a Christmas celebration. I still have years ahead of me for giving, sharing, caring, accepting, loving. I want to live this allotted time in a holiday spirit. What better way to live? For I feel instinctively that it is only this which can give life meaning and offer us our only touch with immortality.